DoggyPedia: All You Need To Know About Dogs

Dog Training for Both Trainers and Owners

Amy Morford

This book is dedicated to everyone who has played a part in my dog journey.

Copyright © 2014 by Speedy Publishing LLC

All rights reserved. No part of this publication may be reproduced, distributed or transmitted in any form or by any means, including photocopying, recording, or other electronic or mechanical methods, without the prior written permission of the publisher, except in the case of brief quotations embodied in critical reviews and certain other noncommercial uses permitted by copyright law. For permission requests, write to the publisher, addressed "Attention: Permissions Coordinator," at the address below.

Speedy Publishing LLC (c) 2014
40 E. Main St., #1156
Newark, DE 19711
www.speedypublishing.co

Ordering Information:
Quantity sales; Special discounts are available on quantity purchases by corporations, associations, and others. For details, contact the "Special Sales Department" at the address above.

-- 1st edition

Manufactured in the United States of America

Table of Contents

Publisher's Notes i

Section A: Puppy Care 1

Chapter 1: How to Make Your Puppy Loving and Obedient 2

Chapter 2: The Right Way to House Train a Puppy 4

Chapter 3: How to Properly Crate Train a Puppy 8

Chapter 4: Make Your Puppy Stop Biting and Mouthing 12

Chapter 5: Stop Puppy Whining and Howling 16

Chapter 6: Teaching Your Puppy to Come When Called 19

Chapter 7: Stop the Jumping Little Puppy 22

Section B: Adult Dog Care and Obedience 25

Chapter 8: Teaching Proper Behavior 26

Chapter 9: Stop Dog Aggression 29

Chapter 10: Separation Anxiety 34

Chapter 11: Nuisance Barking 36

Chapter 12: Submissive Urination 40

Chapter 13: Fear Biting 43

Chapter 14: Digging 47

Section C: Mature & Older Dog Care 49

Chapter 15: How to Help Your Dog Maintain the Right Weight 50

Chapter 16: The Importance of Checkups 54

Chapter 17: Blood Screening 57

Chapter 18: Dental Care For Older Dogs 60

Chapter 19: Treating Arthritis 63

Chapter 20: The Right Exercises for Your Dog's Mind and Body 68

Chapter 21: Why a Massage is Important 71

Chapter 22: Grooming Your Older Dog 75

Meet the Author 78

More Books by Amy Morford 79

Publisher's Notes

Disclaimer

This publication is intended to provide helpful and informative material. It is not intended to diagnose, treat, cure, or prevent any health problem or condition, nor is intended to replace the advice of a physician. No action should be taken solely on the contents of this book. Always consult your physician or qualified health-care professional on any matters regarding your health and before adopting any suggestions in this book or drawing inferences from it.

The author and publisher specifically disclaim all responsibility for any liability, loss or risk, personal or otherwise, which is incurred as a consequence, directly or indirectly, from the use or application of any contents of this book.

Any and all product names referenced within this book are the trademarks of their respective owners. None of these owners have sponsored, authorized, endorsed, or approved this book.

Always read all information provided by the manufacturers' product labels before using their products. The author and publisher are not responsible for claims made by manufacturers.

Print Edition 2014

Section A: Puppy Care

CHAPTER 1: HOW TO MAKE YOUR PUPPY LOVING AND OBEDIENT

You've done your research. You and your family have followed your hearts and you've have finally agreed on a new puppy. Once you have found that puppy, a good vet, and your home has been properly prepared, you can bring your new friend home. You and your family need a plan that everyone can follow. A new puppy needs to be loved, needs boundaries and discipline, and it needs to understand who's boss, yet your puppy should also know it can trust you completely. Training practices should be loving, gentle, positive and consistent among all members of the family to ensure that there is no confusion. Commands need to be agreed upon so that every member of your family is speaking the same language.

Training should always be kept short and fun. Show a puppy what you want, and give praise when the task is performed. Firm and consistent commands along with positive reinforcement and praise will make your puppy understand what's expected, and will reinforce your authority and leadership.

Training needs to happen in different rooms, in different environments, and at different times throughout the day. Be sure to socialize your puppy with other dogs and with people of all ages. Expose your puppy to as many new situations as possible.

A happy and obedient dog has enjoyed a loving and structured life with its family from the start.

Chapter 2: The Right Way to House Train a Puppy

An indoor dog needs to be house trained as quickly as possible. There are things you can do to speed up the process and decrease unpleasant accidents.

Puppies have little control over their bodily functions, so it's important to let them out frequently. Before house training is fully achieved, take your puppy out after naps and at regular intervals. Puppies between the ages of 8 and 12 weeks should be let out every hour. The time between restroom breaks will increase as your puppy ages.

A bathroom or potty area needs to be designated in your yard as your dog's restroom location. Choose a potty command to use for your puppy to associate with going outside. Take your dog out to the designated area in your yard and give your chosen potty command such as "go potty" or "take a break."

Get your puppy into a routine. Always take your puppy out for a potty break first thing in the morning, last thing before bedtime and always after naps. Feed your pup at the same times every day. Monitor your pup's food and water intake and track elimination after eating. Food and water should be restricted a few hours before bedtime. This will reduce accidents and trips outside during the night.

To speed up the house training process, don't give your puppy access to your entire house. Baby gates can be used to confine your dog to a room or a small area. The quickest method you can use to house train a dog and reduce accidents is crate training. Dogs learn to view a crate as their den. It's instinctual for them to keep their den area clean. They will not potty where they sleep. Crated puppies need to be removed from their crates regularly for bathroom breaks, water and play.

When your puppy is inside the house, loose and unrestricted, keep an eye on him. Puppies tend to sneak out of site and relieve themselves, but dogs often alert their owners to their needs. Learn their body language. Whimpering, barking, antsy movements particular to your dog and pawing at doors are all signs that your pet needs to go outside. When you see these behaviors, take your dog out immediately.

If accidents happen, remain calm and do not scold or punish your puppy. Raising your voice and punishing your puppy can cause and create stress and anxiety, which can lead to more accidents. If accidents do occur, be sure to clean them up well to reduce the chances of a repeat accident in the same spot.

Consistency is vital when house training. Be sure everyone involved in potty training is doing the same things and using the same commands. Your dog will become confused if rules are different with every person.

Positive reinforcement is the best way to encourage and praise positive behavior. After your dog relieves himself appropriately, reward him with verbal praise, treats, play and physical affection. This will send the signal that their behavior is a good thing, and they will be more likely to repeat it when you want them to.

Some housing situations such as apartment living make it difficult to house train your dog. Paper training solves this problem. To paper train your pup, contain him or her to one room. A bathroom or other tiled area is ideal. Carpeted floors are best avoided, as they can be hard to clean. Cover the entire floor with newspapers or puppy pads. Your puppy will typically use the restroom in one spot. After a while, you can slightly reduce the amount of paper on the floor. Continue to slowly remove paper. If your pet soils a space outside of the paper, you have decreased the quantity of paper too quickly. Add more, and you can resume paper training.

While it is not ideal, paper training can be used if you will be absent for long periods of time. Try to avoid paper training if you are already in the process of regular house training. Interrupting house training may cause your dog to regress. A better solution is to get a reliable neighbor or relative to take care of your pup when you are away.

House training a puppy is a necessary (and sometimes messy and frustrating) process. Potty training a puppy involves patience, consistency and praise/rewards. If you persistently follow the steps above, your puppy will soon be asking to go outside for bathroom breaks.

Chapter 3: How to Properly Crate Train a Puppy

There are many reasons for pet owners to crate train their puppies. Crate training is an invaluable tool that can assist with potty training and is also a safe haven for your puppy. Some people feel that crate training is cruel, but puppies actually prefer an enclosed space because it makes them feel safe and secure.

With many styles and sizes, choosing the right crate is important. It needs to be big enough for your pup to be able to turn around and stand up in. If the kennel (or crate) is too large, he will have room to relieve himself, defeating the purpose of potty training. If you are concerned about choosing the right crate for your dog, your local pet store can help.

The Process

Introducing your pet to the crate is the first step in training. Make sure you put the crate in a high traffic area in your home. Keeping the crate in the kitchen or living room allows your puppy to see the crate as an upbeat and fun place to be. The placement of the crate should allow your dog visual access to yourself or other members of your household. This will keep your pup from feeling secluded from its pack members.

Encourage your pup to go near the crate. Offer him treats as he gets closer. Put treats inside the crate to get the pup inside. If your puppy seems timid and doesn't want to go all the way inside, don't force him. Let your puppy check out the crate and enter when he feels comfortable. Don't get frustrated, the process may take a few hours or even a few days.

Handle the process incrementally. Put his food dish in the back of his crate while he is still becoming familiar with it. If you are still struggling with your puppy not wanting to go all the way inside, start his food dish just far enough that he doesn't become panicky. With every meal, scoot his food in a little bit further. Soon he will be eating from inside his crate.

Once he is successfully eating inside his crate, shut the door while he eats. Keep a close eye on him because as soon as he is finished with his meal, you need to let him out.

Caution! If your pup starts to whine, you might have left him in too long. After the next meal, try a minute or two less. If he still whines, don't let him out until he stops whining — otherwise he will expect you to let him out any time he whines.

You can extend crate training to help your puppy feel more comfortable when you leave the house.

Start leaving your puppy inside his crate for short time periods (outside of meal times). Here's the step-by-step process:

First, call your puppy over to you, using a treat. Then, direct him to enter his crate. Use commands such as "kennel" or "crate." Reward him with a treat once he enters and you've shut the door. Sit near the crate for five to ten minutes. Leave the room. Make sure you're only absent for a few minutes. Return and sit near the crate again for another few minutes. (Don't excite your puppy — your return shouldn't be an event.) Slowly increase time lengths as you repeat this process over the next couple of days or weeks.

As soon as your puppy can stay quietly in his crate for 30 minutes without you near, you can start leaving the home for periods of time.

Start small and gradually increase the length. Start with 30 minutes. Leaving your puppy in his crate for hours at a time in the beginning of training may cause him to develop separation anxiety. Be sure to put your puppy in his crate 10 to 20 minutes prior to departure.

Never make leaving an ordeal. Using your command ("kennel" or "crate") direct your puppy to his crate, calmly shut the door and reward his compliance with a treat. Upon returning, continue to be calm when letting him out. If you are too excited to see him and show excess affection, he will become anxious every time he is put into his kennel and wonder when you'll be home to give him more love and attention. Staying calm and patient throughout the crate training process will produce the best results. You will have peace of mind knowing your puppy is safe and happy.

Tips & Warnings

Never use the crate to punish your pet. He will begin to associate his kennel as a jail cell instead of a safe place to go.

Never let your puppy out of the crate if he is barking, howling, crying, whining or digging. Wait until your puppy is quiet and calm, and reward the behavior by opening the crate door.

Chapter 4: Make Your Puppy Stop Biting and Mouthing

Puppy biting and chewing is a natural phase, especially when teething. Though it may start out as harmless puppy fun, biting and mouthing should be curbed at an early age. As with any training, the sooner you begin, the easier it will be.

The first step is to teach your puppy bite inhibition, or acceptable force, when using his mouth. A puppy taught to bite with a gentle force is less likely to bite in situations when scared or in pain. Through normal interaction with its litter-mates, a puppy learns bite inhibition. Sometimes during a wrestling match, one puppy will bite another too hard. The bitten puppy yelps and stops playing. The inflictor stops too for a moment, registering that the bite was too hard. Soon they are back to playing but with better control of their bites.

Use the same technique when teaching your puppy how to play gently with humans. Allow him to mouth during play until he bites too hard. At that point, yelp in reaction and stop playing. Avoid pulling your hand away quickly, since this may encourage your puppy to go after it. Instead, allow your hand to go limp. This should elicit a pause in your puppy's reaction. If it doesn't work, try to use a phrase uttered in a more stern tone. Be sure to give positive reinforcement when your puppy does not bite. Resume play and repeat the steps.

If you find yelping alone doesn't stop the behavior try using a time out technique. After a hard bite and a loud yelp, ignore him for 20 seconds. If your puppy comes after you to play, get up and walk away for 20 seconds. When the time out is over, encourage the play session to continue. If rough biting continues, repeat the steps.

The next thing to teach your puppy is that his teeth do not belong on human skin. You can easily teach this behavior through simple methods. If your puppy starts to gnaw on your hand, swap your hand for a chew toy or other acceptable item. Puppies will sometimes get excited when they are being petted and will bite to play. Get him used to your touch in a relaxing way by offering small treats while you pet him with your other hand. Never wave your fingers in his face or slap his face to get him to play. This encourages biting.

Do not encourage rough-house play. Instead, use tug toys to promote non-contact play. Then you can keep the tug toy handy for those biting times. Eventually when he gets the urge he will seek out his tug toy instead of your hands. If you have an ankle biter, stop moving your feet and offer the toy as a distraction. Praise him for tugging the toy and not you. Keeping a wide assortment of things to play with can also help keep him interested in using the toys to chew on. Consider puppy play dates. Socializing your puppy is important to his development. He will use most of his energy with other dogs and will be less likely to use you for rough play.

So you have tried teaching your puppy to bite gently. He's been on a toy shopping spree, and he has some new buddies to play with, but he just can't resist sinking his teeth into your palms. Now what? You can try bitter apple spray products designed to aid you in the training process. Before you interact with your puppy, spray your hands and areas of your clothing with bitter apple. When he mouths the sprayed areas wait for him to stop and react to the taste. Be sure to praise him when he lets go of you. Give the process a few weeks to work.

If all else fails puppy training classes can help immensely. Enlist the help of a certified Professional Dog Trainer (CPDT). You can enroll your pup in a private class for one-on-one attention and/or a group session.

Remember that mouthing is a natural and normal part of your puppy's development, so it's important to be patient and understanding. Never hit your dog for mouthing. This can cause aggression and invoke more biting. Steer clear of any method that causes fear or pain. You do not want to hurt or scare him - you want to teach him through respect, not fear.

Chapter 5: Stop Puppy Whining and Howling

Puppies are similar to children in that they seek constant attention. They bark or whine to get what they want. It's a natural way to get their mother's attention.

Your puppy should grow out of it. However, many do not and they'll need some intervention if the behavior has been allowed to continue.

When you reinforce whining, it will worsen. How do you stop it? First, you need to get to the root of the problem and figure out what your puppy is trying to tell you. The most common reason for whining is that your little puppy just wants some attention. He is likely bored or lonely.

If your dog is uncomfortable, it may set off a whimpering fit. Pain can be a culprit as well. Changing the environment they're used to, such as beginning crate training, may cause a dog to cry. He may need to use the bathroom or already have made a mess. An overabundance of energy, hunger, and thirst could be an issue. Whining can also be caused by separation anxiety. A puppy may whine simply because he wants you to (and knows you will) come to him.

Before starting any training, rule out all possible causes. Make sure your dog has been fed well. Keep to your potty training schedule so that your puppy adjusts to going out to relieve himself at a specific time.

Offer your puppy toys and treats to chew on to give him a distraction. Try taking your puppy out for a walk before bed to burn off extra energy and tire him out. If you suspect something may be medically wrong, visit your vet.

Once you have checked to make sure none of the general triggers are playing a factor, you can implement your plan to remove the unwanted behavior. Remember to always be consistent and persistent.

After making sure your puppy is safe, comfortable, fed, and that he doesn't need a bathroom break, your best course of action is to ignore the whining. It will be difficult, especially the first few nights, but over time the whining will minimize and eventually disappear. Every time you step into the room in response to the dog's whining you are actually rewarding the negative behavior. The puppy thinks he has found a way to get what he wants - you in the room with him. When you give no response, he will soon realize that the tactic doesn't work.

This method has to be consistent. Even one peek in the room by you or anyone else will start you back at the beginning.

Ignoring your puppy may be hard, but you must only give attention when your dog is quiet. When whining starts, go to the door, but do not walk in to the room. Use a firm voice to tell the puppy to be quiet. As soon as he becomes quiet, enter the room and offer a small treat and verbal praise. This is a slow process, but eventually your puppy will associate being quiet with positive reinforcement from you.

CHAPTER 6: TEACHING YOUR PUPPY TO COME WHEN CALLED

Teaching your puppy to come when called is one of the most important things to teach your dog. This command is easy to train.

To properly teach a puppy to come when called, we need to convince him or her that no matter how much fun he or she may be having, if the dog obeys the *come* command when his or her master calls, life will be even better. This is positive reinforcement at its best.

A very good way to teach your puppy to come when called is to use treats. (If you are giving your dog treats all the time, they won't be as meaningful or effective, so it is important to not overindulge.)

Hold a small piece of food like a small piece of hot dog and then call to him with the *come* command. Your puppy will see the treat and will come running for it. Practice before mealtimes so the dog will be hungry and more motivated to get the food. Give just a small amount, so that he will stay hungry and want more. When your puppy follows the *come* command give him or her a treat and praise. Gradually reduce the number of treats given with each practice session.

When it's time to go for walks, you can also use those moments for practice.

Give the *come* command, then grab the leash and shake it; if the dog does not come immediately, put the leash away and ignore your puppy. The puppy will soon get the message that if he or she does not respond quickly, a walk outside will not happen.

Practice each command consistently. Dogs like routine, and they become conditioned to respond to stimulus, such as a promise of food or a trip outside. It is also important to use the same command each time you call your dog. You may say "come," or say the dogs name with the command. The important thing is to teach a routine. If you change the command, the dog will become confused and training will suffer.

Teach your puppy to come when called using rewards for good behavior. Avoid the temptation to punish your puppy when he or she does not come to you after being called. It sends the wrong message and teaches your puppy to actually avoid you.

CHAPTER 7: STOP THE JUMPING LITTLE PUPPY

Puppies naturally jump when they are excited. A jumping little puppy can rip up stockings, snag pants, or worse, snag bare legs or arms. They jump on furniture, knock things over, and can create a real mess, especially if their paws are muddy or wet.

And that jumping can cause injury to your puppy or to others. This is especially true if the puppy is of a larger breed. Constant jumping can cause strain and injury to the developing muscles and joints in his or her legs.

How to Stop Puppy from Jumping on Guests

The reason puppies jump on guests is not to show aggression but to say hello.

Keep your puppy's leash handy whenever company comes. Clip on the leash before answering the door.

Walk the leashed puppy to the door with you. Hold the leash back from the guest and when the puppy tries to jump, pull the leash toward you and say, "off!" in a firm voice. Rub the puppy's head and say, "Good off!" immediately after it stops. You can also use the *sit* command for this. Remember to say, "Good sit!" immediately after the order is obeyed. If he or she sits for a second or two and then tries to jump again, repeat the command and stand on the leash so that the puppy cannot move further.

When your puppy has remained in the sit position for a few moments, allow your guest to give your puppy positive reinforcement through verbal praise or petting. If this excites your puppy and causes jumping, repeat the "off" command in a firm voice and pull the leash back.

Repeat this as often as necessary. Be careful not to waver. This may take some time and patience, but it will work if you do it consistently.

In time you will not need to use the leash. With proper training, your dog will understand how to behave when guests come to visit.

How to Stop Your Puppy from Jumping on You

One way to put a stop to jumping is to grab the puppy's front paws as soon as it jumps up on you. Don't hold the paws with enough force to hurt your puppy, use just enough to make it want to get away. Use the *off* or *sit* command. Reward him or her with verbal praise, and with a pat on the head or a treat each time he or she obeys. If you keep doing this every time the puppy attempts to jump up on you, he or she should quickly get the message and stop jumping.

Many puppies will stop jumping on you if you ignore them by turning your back every time they attempt to jump. Do this each time the puppy jumps up, and he should soon get the message. Each time the puppy sits down and stops jumping on you, reward your puppy with verbal praise, a pat on the head and/or a treat.

There is one more technique - whenever the puppy tries to jump up on you, lift your knee gently to block the space between you and the puppy. Use the *off* command as you lift your knee. Never jab your knee into the puppy's body; simply use it to block the jump. As the puppy moves away from you and sets all four paws on the ground, say "Good off!" Reward your puppy each time he obeys the command.

These training methods will stop the jumping little puppy and produce a well-behaved dog.

Section B: Adult Dog Care and Obedience

Chapter 8: Teaching Proper Behavior

A well-behaved dog is the result of good treatment and consistent, positive training. Make sure you bring home the right breed for your lifestyle. The right dog for your home, family and life will make a big difference in the training process.

If you lack adequate time to train your dog, enroll him or her in obedience classes. Obedience classes will not only teach your dog, but teach *you* how to train your dog. Good obedience training will teach your dog basic commands such as *sit, down, come,* and *stay*, as well as how to walk on a leash and behave around other dogs. Even if your dog is just a puppy, it is important to take it out and let it spend plenty of time around other people and dogs, as this will greatly improve its socialization skills.

After completing an obedience class, stay consistent in your training. Be certain to reward good behavior and *avoid* rewarding bad behavior.

One common thing dogs tend to do is pull on a leash. Many owners let their dogs pull on the leash and keep walking, or they choose to use a retractable leash. This does much more harm than good.

A retractable leash sends the message that if your dog pulls on the leash, it will be able to go where it wants to go. It is best to purchase a shorter leash and train your dog to walk next to you. The instant your dog pulls on the leash, either stop walking completely, or turn around and walk in the other direction.

Another common example of negative behavior is a dog darting out the house whenever the door is open, or jumping all over guests who walk through the door. The best way to remedy this situation is by teaching your dog a solid *sit, stay* command each time you need to open the door. While training, place your dog in a sitting stay and pretend you are going to open the door. If your dog leaves the sit position, immediately stop what you are doing and repeat the command until he or she obeys.

Go through the motions of opening the door and reward your dog for sitting still, stretching the period between the door opening and the reward each time your dog is successful. Eventually you can ask someone else to knock on the door and pretend to be a guest. Reward your dog for staying calmly seated.

This principle of rewarding only good behavior and refusing to reward bad behavior can be applied to any sort of misbehavior from your dog. It is important to remember to be consistent and calm in your training, and always see it as an opportunity to encourage positive behavior.

CHAPTER 9: STOP DOG AGGRESSION

There are effective strategies when dealing with dog aggression. These strategies are based on the following:

- Teaching puppies not to be aggressive is easier than teaching older dogs to unlearn their aggressive responses.
- Aggressiveness should never be used to treat aggressiveness.
- Positive reinforcement methods are the most effective for training purposes.
- Aggressive dogs need to learn alternative, acceptable behaviors.

Dogs show aggression for different reasons. Some dogs are aggressive about protecting their food and toys. Some are aggressive when they come in contact with other dogs, and other may be aggressive against people who invade their yard, home, or space. Aggressive dogs can be dangerous when they are not under the control of their owners. When and how your dog displays aggression will determine the steps you take to stop the behavior.

Teaching Puppies Not to be Aggressive

Aggression prevention strategies can be used at an early age to help prevent the development of aggressive responses.

Rules and Boundaries

Puppies and dogs need rules and boundaries. Some trainers suggest that a puppy should be kept on a leash whenever he's out of his crate. That way, behaviors such as house breaking, jumping on people, or chewing furniture can be stopped immediately. Whatever rules and boundaries you set, make sure to consistently follow through. If the puppy is not allowed on the furniture, never allow the puppy on the furniture.

Obedience Training

Obedience training should be started immediately to teach commands such as *sit, down, come,* and *stay*. The sessions should be short but frequent, up to three times a day. Obedience training asserts your authority and helps establish respect.

Socialization

It is important to only introduce a puppy to new people, places, and situations as you monitor the experience. The socialization experience is critical. It shapes the way your dog views life - these experiences teach him or her to be comfortable with new experiences. Many trainers believe that improper socialization is the root problem behind unprovoked dog aggression.

Positive Reinforcement

Puppies, like children, respond to praise and treats. With positive reinforcement, your puppy will be more likely to repeat the behavior you desire. Positive reinforcement is the most powerful methods you can use to affect behavior.

Food Aggression

Some dogs guard their food by stiffening their posture, glaring, growling, and not allowing you to get near the food dish. This type of aggression can lead to guarding other things in the house that the dog feels possessive of, such as dog toys, beds, or anything else. Dogs that growl over food or dog treats should be taken seriously as this is not normal behavior. Some dogs show food aggression against other dogs or cats. This type of aggression does not normally shift over to aggression against people, but still should not be tolerated.

Use positive training techniques to stop the behavior. (Negative training techniques such as punishment or physical controls can lead to snapping and biting.) Continue obedience training and teach your puppy or dog two commands using behavior modification and positive reinforcement. "Leave it," and "Drop it."

The training for these commands is similar to teaching your puppy or dog other commands, but they specifically relate to food. Tell your dog to leave it, and rewarded him with praise and a much more loved treat when he does.

Aggression against Other Dogs

Some breeds of dogs are more dominant than others and don't want to share their space. Some dogs are defensive, scared, or shy. Some pets are genetically bred to be more aggressive. Dogs that are aggressive against other dogs can be trained using desensitization, trust, and positive reinforcement. Desensitization is a widely used behavior modification technique to change an animal's emotional response to a stimulus. In this case, the stimulus is other dogs and the response is the aggression.

The process involves initially exposing your pet to the stimulus from such a great distance that the aggressive behavior is not produced. The dog is verbally praised and rewarded with a treat. The training continues, bringing the dog closer and closer to the stimulus. The goal is to avoid provoking the aggressive behavior, even as the intensity of the stimulus increases.

Aggressive Dogs

If you have moments where you are afraid of your dog and afraid for others, take it seriously. Even the smallest signs of aggression could escalate into serious problems. Aggressive animals are a huge liability and need to be strictly monitored. Do not be embarrassed or ashamed to seek out professional help.

Animal Behaviorists are trained to help dogs that exhibit aggressive behavior. When the professional and a dog's owner work together using positive reinforcement, remarkable positive changes can occur.

Chapter 10: Separation Anxiety

One of the most common problems owners experience with new dogs is separation anxiety - when a dog feels very anxious when left alone. Indicators that your dog is suffering from separation anxiety include: destroying property, excessive barking, self-destructive behavior, and inappropriate urination and defecation.

Dogs suffering from separation anxiety may also whine, bark, cry, howl, dig, excessively lick themselves, or chew and scratch at the door the entire time their owners are away.

Crating your dog is a great way to help alleviate some of the strain that separation anxiety imposes on your dog. This new enclosure gives them a sense of protection from the outside world.

To help your dog become more at ease with your departure and absence, always greet your dog in a very calm and gentle voice. Arousing excitement in your dog when you return home causes them more distress when you leave them. If you give them a short and calm greeting when you return home, this will train them to know that it is okay for you to be gone.

Make sure your dog is getting enough physical activity. Schedule exercise before your departure for the day. Going on walks or runs will help burn off excess energy, and a tired dog will generally sleep away the time its owner is away. Make your absence a positive experience by rewarding your dog with desirable treats, rawhides and chew toys. The treats initially serve as a distraction to your departure, but eventually your dog will associate your absence with a treat or reward.

Dogs that suffer from separation anxiety will always suffer from it. Correcting separation anxiety is an ongoing process. As you see improvements in your dog the process becomes easier, but stress and the disruption of routines can revert your dog to its old behavior.

Chapter 11: Nuisance Barking

Dogs bark. They were born to bark. Dogs bark when there is danger, when they need something, and, unfortunately, just because they can. While barking is a natural behavior, it is one that can cause great duress and even legal problems. You can spare your neighbors by quieting your dog's nuisance barking.

As you train your dog, don't forget positive reinforcement. Avoid yelling, as your dog may think you are barking with him or her. Once you set boundaries and rules, maintain them. Improperly enforced rules confuse your dog more than yelling. Keep these things in mind to get the most out of your training.

Before you can stop a dog from barking, you need to understand why it barks. Separation anxiety, boredom, aggression, and territorial issues are all potential triggers.

If your dog is primarily barking when you are absent, then separation anxiety may be to blame.

Bored dogs dig, chew, and also bark. Your dog has a boredom issue if he or she is destructive and disruptive. Boredom is different from separation anxiety because bored dogs that bark want your attention. Bored dogs engage in their negative behaviors even when you are present.

Aggressive dogs are characterized by bared teeth, growling, raised hackles, and threatening postures. They bark at anything they see as dangerous.

The last category is a dog set off by things like pedestrians and squirrels. Anything they see, they bark at. They are territorial and will bark to protect their home.

Once you've identified the source of the nuisance barking, it is time to treat it.

If your pet suffers from separation anxiety, ignore his or her frantic barking both when you leave and when you enter the house. Consoling your anxious dog reinforces and rewards the behavior. By reducing the importance of leaving, you ease your dog's fear. He or she will no longer see your departure as an earth-shattering, irreversible event. You can also take away some of your dog's nervous tension through exercise. Take your dog on a long walk before you go. A tired dog doesn't have the energy to bark.

Dogs need entertainment, just like you. Exercise your dog regularly, and you should see a reduction in barking. Also provide your pet with a variety of toys. This will keep your dog entertained when you are not there. Take your dog out for socialization with other dogs and people. Socialization is stimulating, and because dogs are pack animals, it is important for them to associate with other dogs. Dog daycares are a good alternative. The daycare removes your dog from their typical environment and effectively cures their boredom.

Aggressive dogs can be very troublesome, if not dangerous. A muzzle can be used if your dog poses a threat to others. (Do not leave a muzzle on for extended periods of time.) Contact a professional trainer to get help correcting aggressive behavior. Always restrict an aggressive dog's access to other people and animals.

A territorial dog that is not overly aggressive can be dealt with by limiting what they can see. Territorial dogs often rush to windows to bark at things. To dissuade this behavior, try closing your blinds. Your dog will not bark at things it can't see. If you don't want to close your blinds, you can teach your dog a *quiet* command. Pick a word to use. Each time your dog barks, firmly say this word. Reward them with a treat after they fall silent. Your dog will learn to associate being quiet with positive rewards.

Bark collars are another option. Bark collars are popular because they are automated, and they work. A bark collar interrupts barking behavior with discomfort. The vibration from your dog's vocal cords activates the collar. There are three different types of bark collars to choose from. Audio bark collars release a sharp noise to distract your dog. Chemical collars spray citronella at the sound of a bark. An electrical collar (e-collar) uses small amounts of electrical stimulation.

Nuisance dog barking is frustrating and annoying. Pay attention to your dog's specific needs and make sure your dog is not barking due to injury, hunger or thirst. Repetitive training, consistency and exercise, will assist you in ending your dog's nuisance barking.

Chapter 12: Submissive Urination

Submissive urination is a habitual behavior based on the personality of the dog and how he or she chooses to interact with the world. Dogs urinate in submission in order to say that they accept the power of a person or another animal. Submissive urination occurs in both male and female dogs. There are ways to curb this response and stop submissive urination altogether.

Ending submissive urination is not something that you will be able to do quickly. Your puppy or dog is going to need to be trained to respond differently in various scenarios. Breaking this behavior will take time, but it can be done.

It's recommended that you make an appointment to see your dog's veterinarian to rule out underlying health problems if the problem is frequent.

Age, just as in human adults, can play a role in this kind of behavior. Much like elderly people, older pets can develop incontinence issues that are outside of their control. They simply void their bowels and bladder without even realizing it, even doing it in their sleep. This does not fall under the banner of submissive urination, but rather a medical condition.

Another issue is a urinary tract infection. This condition in pets causes them to release small amounts of urine regularly. It is often something they can attempt to control, but fail to do so. You can often spot this condition by noticing an excessive licking of genitalia.

If you have determined that your dog's behavior is not a result of a medical condition, you can begin working on reversing the problem.

Reduce Excitement

Urination occurs often when a dog is excited, and may be a particular problem when meeting people or other pets. Reducing excitement can help curb voiding of the bladder.

Train your dog to sit, and practice the command when interacting with anyone new, or even when your dog or pup is greeting you when you've come back home for the day. This is a two-part process - it gives your dog something to remember to do when he or she meets someone new or is greeting you. Secondly, this also calms your dog down and helps your dog to relax so that the uncontrollable urge to urinate is less pressing.

Of course you can also avoid interacting with your dog when you get home, until he or she has calmed down. This can help your dog to understand that this is what you want him to do. Your dog will learn to calm down in order to interact with you each day. When you finally do interact with your pet, make sure that you are calm and do not rile them up.

When your dog submissively urinates, it is important not to yell at or punish your dog. This can even make the problem worse because the dog sees you as an even bigger threat. It is wise to avoid any eye contact or physical contact with your dog if you think he is about to submissively urinate. This allows the dog to associate its urination with a lack of response from you, and can aid in stopping the habit.

Monitor your dog's water intake and be sure you are taking your dog outside on a regular basis. Lavish your dog with verbal praise and treats when he goes outside. This positively reinforces good behavior and should encourage him to relieve himself outside.

Dogs with low confidence and dogs that have been physically abused are the most likely candidates to suffer from submissive urination. Puppies and dogs under a year old that are showing submissive urination behavior can grow out of it with a little bit of guidance and positive reinforcement from you.

Chapter 13: Fear Biting

While every dog has his own quirks and characteristics, biting is not an acceptable under any circumstance, other than in self-protection or to protect its owner. When you have a dog that demonstrates serious aggression, you have a problem that requires immediate attention.

Most dogs have a reason for biting, although it may not be obvious to the owner, or to the person on the receiving end of the bite. Dogs operate on instinct and habit; unless there is a serious behavioral issue with the animal, owner training should resolve any issue with biting. (If the dog does have problems, such as learned aggression or exposure to abuse resulting in reflexive biting, other professional options should be explored.)

First, determine the motivation for biting. This should be done through analysis of the dog's history of aggression, and he should be kept away from people he could potentially harm until he is under control. While this may take time, it's important that the dog not be completely isolated in a way he perceives as punishment, as this can exacerbate his negative behavior. Simply keep him out of direct contact with anyone except his (family and trainer, if necessary) and get to work.

Possessive instinct frequently prompts aggressive behavior, and can lead to a quick snap of the dog's jaw. If you determine that your dog is biting due to a possessive streak, teach him the *wait* command. You can begin with a toy or a treat; just make sure it's something he really wants. (Do not practice this before mealtimes). Start with something fun that the animal already sees as community property, such as something you toss around and play tug-of-war with.

Drop the item on the floor or ground, and tell your dog to wait, in a firm and commanding voice. By practicing this repeatedly, he will learn that your instructions supersede his desire to possess or control. Offer positive reinforcement for his good behavior, and when you pet him, move your hands closer and closer to his neck and jaw, so that he is less threatened by something going near his mouth. He will learn that he has nothing to worry about, and that no one wants to take things from him.

Fear and anxiety also contribute to a dog's motivation to bite, and these emotions can be more difficult to contain. When a dog bites out of fear, he feels threatened in some way. Therefore, desensitizing him with exposure to a variety of social situations is crucial.

Keep your dog on a short leash and bring him to different places where there are people. Sit quietly together and simply let the animal observe and absorb. With a few reassuring pats on the back from you, he should start to relax and feel more comfortable. As he adjusts, walk him closer to people and other animals, holding the leash firmly and commanding him to *heel* or *leave it*. Provided he maintains his composure, bring your dog even closer to others, and repeat this practice on a daily basis. Gradually, the two of you should be able to work your way up to positive interactions with strangers.

Being in his own yard may provoke more intense emotional responses in your dog, even as he progresses in other social settings. Since dogs are territorial by nature, more intense conditioning may be needed on "his" property. Go out of your way to introduce him to regular visitors. This will reassure your dog that there is no danger. Make sure that anyone who comes onto your property, such as the mailman or maintenance personnel, knows and uses the dog's name.

Although using treats may help your dog become friendlier with strangers, handling food while your dog is aggressive can be risky.

Proper introduction and socialization are the best ways of helping your dog navigate his emotions in social settings. Conditioning him with repeated exposure should reinforce what you teach and lead to more passive greeting habits.

There may be unforeseen factors influencing your dog's aggressive behavior. Pain, for instance, will cause any animal to lash out, especially at strangers. If he is not responding well to your training efforts, bring him to your veterinarian for an evaluation. Since any dog that is not neutered or spayed may be inclined toward greater aggression the procedure will most likely be recommended by the doctor if it's something you have not yet taken care of. All other possible health related issues should be eliminated.

If all else fails and your pet continues to demonstrate dangerous tendencies, consult with a professional obedience trainer. This may be the only way to curb your dog's aggression and create a stable environment in which he can learn to exist normally.

Be aware that successfully training your dog may take some time, and that the process can become expensive. Make sure the professional you hire is highly reputable and has the necessary experience to help your dog learn to adjust and overcome his issues.

For obvious reasons, biting should never be tolerated, and the sooner you nip this problem in the bud, the better off everyone will be.

Chapter 14: Digging

Digging is an annoying negative canine behavioral trait. It results in ruined landscaping, holes in the yard and holes under fencing, which can lead to your dog roaming the neighborhood.

Digging is an instinctive behavior for dogs. Your dog's urge to dig is normal and healthy. It is a natural instinct for a dog to hide a bone or some other prized possession.

Problem digging is a result of your dog being bored.

When your dog is left home alone, he becomes bored. To entertain himself and pass the time, your dog digs. If your dog suffers from separation anxiety, it may dig to alleviate stress.

Make sure your dog has lots of chew toys, treats and acceptable diversions to keep him entertained and out of trouble. Be sure your dog is getting exercise appropriate for its size and age. A happy dog is a tired dog, and a tired dog is less likely to get into mischief.

If your dog destroys landscaping from destructive digging, do not replace the area if you do not plan on relocating the dog to a different area of the yard or plan on kenneling him. This only sets you and your dog up for failure. Your dog will repeat the destructive digging behavior as many times as you replace the landscaping.

Kenneling a dog on a concrete slab will immediately control the digging behavior. The initial cost of the kennel will be money well spent when landscaping and yard items no longer have to be replaced on a regular basis.

Occasional digging issues can be stopped by removing temptations and removing your dog from the environment, as well as catching your dog digging in the act and discouraging the behavior.

Section C: Mature & Older Dog Care

Chapter 15: How to Help Your Dog Maintain the Right Weight

It is very important for your dog to maintain the right weight. There are several things you can do to help ensure that they do. First, talk to your vet to find out what the ideal weight should be for your dog. It can vary based on breed, gender, and even age.

Daily Exercise

As a puppy, your dog is going to be hyper and active. All of that exercise is good! However, as your dog matures, he or she will likely become less active. Daily exercise is still important, but you may need to motivate your dog to take part. Playing with your dog, taking your dog for a walk, and encouraging your dog to move is important. Keeping your dog active can help you with your daily exercise, too!

Give your dog plenty of room for roaming and movement. If you have to put your dog on a leash in the yard from time to time, build a run so that he or she isn't stuck in only one small location. You can also fence a smaller portion of the yard from the overall size in order to allow your dog to move about freely. For the winter, you may want to purchase a doggy treadmill that can be used indoors.

When your dog needs to lose weight, be sure to increase the amount of exercise over a period of time. You need to make sure you don't overexert your dog. By adding an extra block or two each time you take him or her out for a walk, those extra calories burned will add up very quickly.

Go to a dog park and toss a ball or a Frisbee. He or she will love chasing it and bringing it back to you. Healthy play is a wonderful way for you to bond with your pet.

If your dog has limitations due to health issues, talk to your vet. Perhaps you can take your dog to the local lake for a swim, or try other forms of low impact exercise.

Balanced Diet

It can be tempting to feed your dog leftovers or to give him a nibble of what you are consuming. Human foods are often high in fat and they are hard for your dog digest. Give your dog the foods that are recommended by your vet. When your dog has the food that offers them vital vitamins and nutrients they will have more energy, burn fat, and be healthier overall.

Portion Control

Be careful not to feed your dog too much. Some breeds are more prone to eating just because food is available to them. Talk to your vet to identify the volume of food per day that your dog should eat. Divide it into two equal portions each day and feed your dog one in the morning and the other at night.

Watch the treats, as they can add lots of additional calories that your dog doesn't need. If you are training your dog, go with morsels instead of full-sized treats for your dog. If you give treats, give something nutritious. You can also replace treats with some fun toys that your dog will really enjoy.

Multiple Dogs

When you have more than one dog, it can become more of a challenge to help them maintain the right weight. It's important to make sure each of them gets the right amount of exercise daily. You also need to make sure one of them isn't consuming more than their share of the food. Using your home's layout, you can segregate feeding areas.

Routine Checkups

Make sure you schedule routine checkups with the vet. This will help to identify any health issues (including extra weight) early on. Prevention and early intervention are key to helping your dog maintain a better overall weight. Some dogs do have health problems that can make it harder for them to lose weight, such as thyroid problems, diabetes, arthritis, or heart disease. Your vet can perform a complete assessment and help you to create a realistic plan of action.

Chapter 16: The Importance of Checkups

Routine preventative care is just as important for dogs as it is for people. Even if your pet appears and acts completely normal, it needs to be seen by the vet regularly. An annual exam will keep your dog's health at its best, improve quality of life, and ensure that your dog lives a long, healthy life.

A routine annual exam can help pinpoint potential illnesses or warning signs of issues that may affect your dog today or in the near future.

A typical veterinarian exam begins at the nose and travels down to the tail. The veterinarian will examine the nose for any discharge. Discharge or rhinitis is a common symptom of many diseases that affect dogs.

Next, the veterinarian will look at the dog's eyes. A healthy dog's eyes should be bright and active. A dog's eyes are normally full of life, and that translates into health and happiness. Dull or lifeless eyes are a concern. They can indicate internal parasites, stress, or some other serious condition.

The doctor will also check for debris of discharge near the eyes. Infections in the eyes can begin with the smallest amount of discharge. Any eye infections must be caught as early as possible so that they can be treated. Eye infections can be contagious to people as well as other pets.

Next is the mouth. The mouth is examined for irregularities like scrapes, cuts, or lumps. Any bumps or lumps on or around the dog's jaw can indicate an allergic reaction to an insect bite, an abscessed tooth, or an oral tumor. The teeth and gums are also examined, ensuring that teeth are clean and healthy. If the teeth appear discolored or there is a lot of tarter build up, then the doctor will recommend a cleaning or scaling. Unhealthy gums may be a sign of anemia.

Dog's ears can collect bacteria that can lead to infections and smelly odors. A vet can catch any infection problems early.

Next, the veterinarian examines the chest using a stethoscope. Sounds of congestion must be taken care of right away. They can be a sign of more serious health issues like heartworm or distemper.

The doctor will also listen to the heart to ensure that there are no abnormalities. Irregular heartbeats or other problems can signal heart disease. Early detection can help the doctor determine the best treatment plan. Prompt treatment and constant monitoring can help your dog lead a normal life.

The vet will then look at the coat and skin of the dog. The skin is the largest organ of the body for people and dogs alike. The veterinarian will look for fleas, ticks, and other insects, and any cuts or scrapes. A shiny coat means a healthy dog. A dull coat means the dog is battling some illness.

The veterinarian will next look at the dog's stomach region. The doctor will feel the abdominal and the groin area to ensure that there are no lumps, swelling, or infections. If the dog cries out or moves in what appears to be pain, there could be issues.

The vet will examine the spine and tail of the dog to look for any orthopedic issues. Then, the vet will examine the legs and paws - ensuring there is no damage, cuts, swelling, or infection.

Signs and symptoms of a potential illness can go undetected without an annual exam. By the time the symptoms are noticed, it could be too late for a full recovery. Save your dog from unnecessary pain and discomfort. Save yourself from unnecessary emotional pain and guilt, and be sure to schedule annual visits for your dog.

CHAPTER 17: BLOOD SCREENING

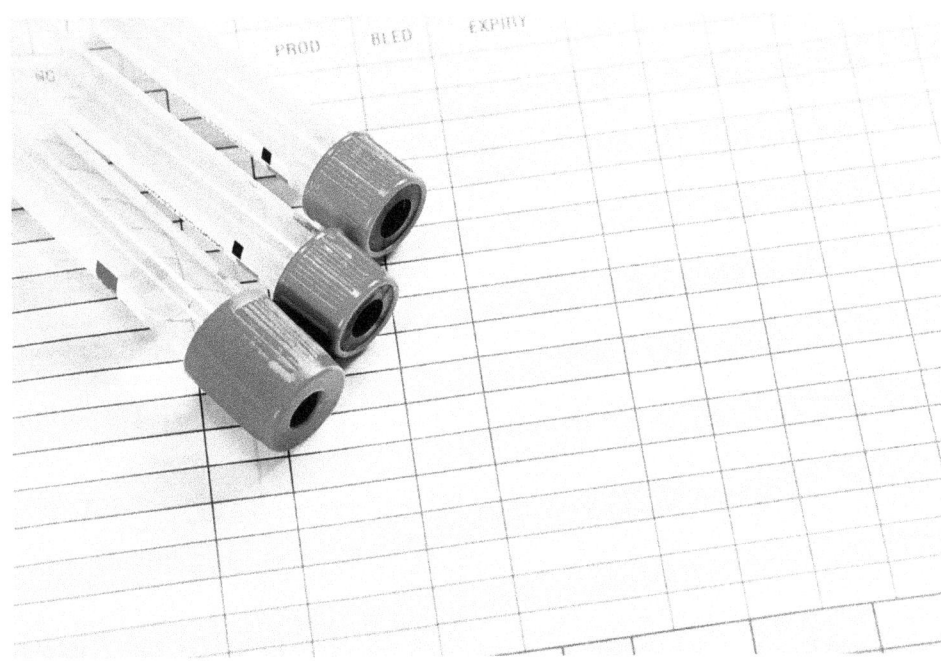

Any dog lover will tell you that one of the hardest parts of being a dog lover is watching a beloved friend get old. Our dogs experience some of the same challenges humans do as they age.

As mentioned in the previous chapter, one of the best ways to help our dogs stay healthy is with yearly wellness exams, and blood screening is a crucial part. The most basic test is the CBC, or complete blood count of the red and white blood cells in a specific volume of blood.

The doctor will be primarily interested in your dog's level of red blood cells. Low red blood count can indicate anemia and your doctor will need to treat this affliction early. The CBC test should be done at least once a year, possibly more if there is a health problem or any change in behavior or personality. If a dog is advanced in age, the test will be done twice a year to properly monitor overall health.

Your vet may also recommend a chemistry profile. It covers properties such as enzymes, glucose, proteins, electrolytes, cholesterol, and other substances produced by the internal organs, which determines organ function. This is a test done only once a year on a healthy, happy dog, but can be done more if needed if the dog is currently dealing with heartworm, for instance, or if the dog is undergoing treatment for cancer.

Another test a vet could run is the serum chemistry panel. It specifically measures the liver, kidney, pancreas, and other organ functions. It can help the doctor go a step further in identifying an issue, such as the onset of kidney failure.

Any surgeries need to be proceeded by a CBC and at least one of the tests above to make sure that a dog is healthy enough to undergo surgery.

Blood tests may also shed light on why a dog is gaining weight and failing to lose it. The test can help determine if there is an underlying factor contributing to the weight gain.

Something to keep in mind is that dogs, like people, have their own normal. Therefore what may fall within the typical normal range may not be normal for your dog. Here, your vet is a valuable asset.

It is hard for any of us to watch a beloved pet age, but with the help of a good vet and routine blood tests such as a chemistry panel and CBC, you can help your dog to stay healthy, happy, and fit for many years to come.

Chapter 18: Dental Care For Older Dogs

With age comes change. As the dog's activity begins to slow down, his chances for more health concerns may begin to increase. There are actions that owners can take to help slow down the effects of aging on their beloved pets.

As the dog ages, the dog's needs, dietary requirements, and exercise will change. Owners may not be aware of all the changes, but it is an owner's responsibility to know how to adjust the care he/she provides his or her dog. It is also an owner's responsibility to notice changes in behavior or appearance that could be cause for concern. After all, the dog is relying on his or her owner to provide a healthy, safe, and optimal living environment.

Dogs do not all enter the senior stage of life at the same time, but most will reach the elder stage between seven and ten years of age. As the dog ages, owners must maintain oral hygiene along with diet and overall fitness.

Dental hygiene is important because tartar and plaque buildup is unhealthy and potentially dangerous. If teeth are left unclean, the buildup can lead to other health issues.

Cleanings can be professionally done at the veterinarian's office, but they can also be done at home by brushing the teeth with toothpaste that is specially created for dogs.

Not many dogs enjoy the process of brushing, so it should be slowly introduced. Keep in mind that the dog will be less likely to cooperate if brushing takes too long or if the dog is restrained.

The best approach is to make the process short and calm. Keeping the process positive will help maintain the dog's attention. If the brushing is kept short, then the dog will not have much of an opportunity to run off.

Begin by introducing the action of brushing without actually brushing. For instance, make sure your dog is comfortably seated and rub the dog's teeth and mouth with the tip of your finger.

The finger can be dipped into a chicken or beef broth-like solution.

The next time the brushing is set to occur, wrap a finger or two in gauze and rub each tooth in a circular motion. This will provide the dog with an understanding of how the brushing is completed and how it will feel. Maintain a cool and calm attitude and offer plenty of praise and positive communication.

The dog is then ready for a soft toothbrush. A soft brush designed specifically for dogs is recommended. The toothpaste you use should always be veterinarian approved. Never use toothpaste made for people.

Diet also plays a role in dental care. As dogs mature, their nutritional needs change. Specially formulated food for dental health is available, and the doctor can help explain which is best and how much should be given to your dog.

Taking care of an older dog is different than caring for a puppy. Dog owners should consult with their veterinarians to help ensure the best care possible is being provided.

Chapter 19: Treating Arthritis

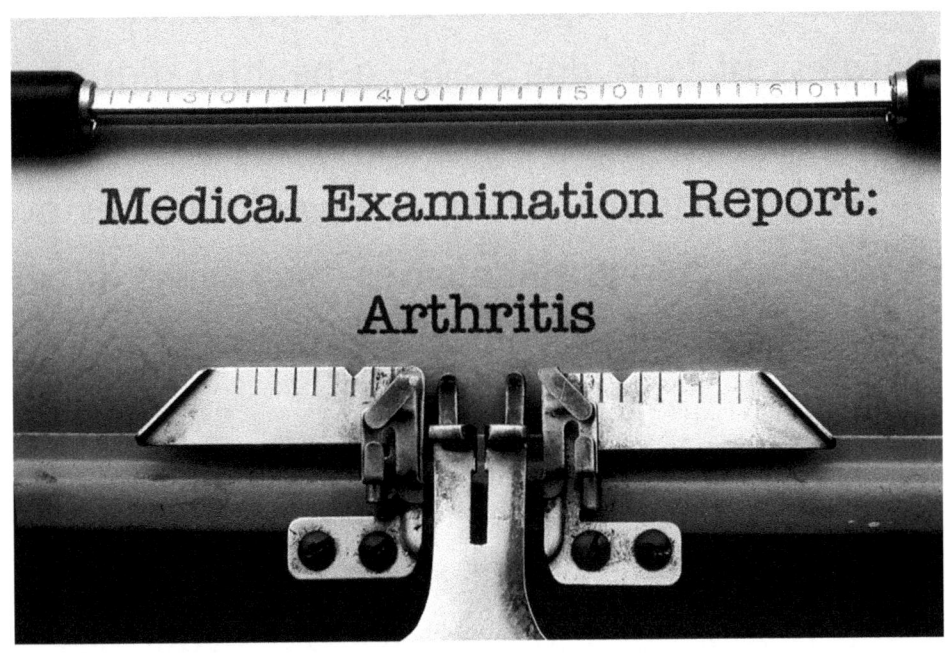

The Silent Pain of Canine Arthritis

According to the Arthritis Foundation, one in five adult dogs in the United States lives with the pain of arthritis. Canine arthritis is the most common cause of chronic pain treated by veterinarians. Subtle signs that your dog is suffering from arthritis may first appear to be due to age or injury. Often, the dog will lose interest in play, or favor a limb. You may notice a limp that seems to come and go, joint stiffness, or difficulty standing and a reluctance to jump. Your dog may begin to sleep more than usual, seem less alert, experience behavioral changes and gain weight. Any of these signs should be taken seriously and should be discussed with your veterinarian. Early detection is the best way you can help your pet in managing arthritis pain.

Pet Specific Therapy

Your dog is as unique as you are. Similar to osteoarthritis in humans, canine arthritis needs to be addressed on an individual basis. Regardless of your dog's age, a healthy diet and routine exercise will help to maintain an optimum weight, which will reduce the pain of arthritis. Being overweight places even more strain on sore joints, and in some cases, may cause inflammation. Your veterinarian will assess your dog's condition and prescribe a drug treatment to manage the pain.

It's important that you monitor your dog's behavior as the drug treatments build up in his or her system. Discuss any symptoms with your vet. Is your dog more active? Does your dog still seem to be experiencing pain? You veterinarian can adjust the dosage or change the medication based on your dog's progress. NSAIDS or nonsteroidal anti-inflammatory drugs are the most common drug treatment for canine arthritis.

Hydrotherapy

Water therapy, or hydrotherapy, has been shown to help some dogs manage arthritis and build stronger joint muscles. Obese dogs benefit from the "weightless" exercise hydrotherapy offers by keeping some of the strain off their joints as they work their muscles. This no-impact workout also helps improve cardiovascular health. Discuss hydrotherapy with your veterinarian, and if it's not offered at the clinic, he or she may be able to suggest a treatment center in your area. Some pet owners have used backyard pools and Jacuzzi tubs successfully, but temperature control can be difficult.

What You Can Do

Diet supplements designed to build joint health and flexibility such as glucosamine, chondroitin sulfate and omega fatty acids can be purchased over the counter as pills or edible food products and have been shown to relieve pain in canines suffering from arthritis.

(Never give your dog medications intended for human use or consumption. Some over the counter medications such as acetaminophen and ibuprofen are toxic to dogs.)

Topical pain relievers such as muscle rubs and creams may irritate your dog's skin and cause an allergic reaction. Hot or cold compresses can be beneficial, but only under the advisement of your veterinarian. Never use an electric heating pad on your dog unless you plan to watch your dog the entire time the pad is being used. Heating pads can cause burns, and a dog may chew on the cord, either of which could lead to serious injury.

General Hygiene

As with any living being, general hygiene plays a role in health and wellness. It's very important that you pay close attention to the feet of arthritic dogs and keep their nails properly trimmed. Any foot ailment can cause undue strain on the joints and lead to arthritic pain and inflammation. Check your dog routinely for fleas and ticks, ear mites, and any pests that could cause them to scratch. If the dog scratches while standing it can place undue strain on the opposite hip or leg joints.

If your dog is sleeping or laying down more than usual, check for "hot spots" minor skin irritations caused by body heat and pressure to one side of the body. These spots are similar to bed sores in humans, but are harder to spot under a dog's coat. Never hesitate to call your veterinarian if you notice any health or hygiene issue that might be adding further pain or suffering to your dog's condition.

Managing Canine Arthritis

Effective treatment of your dog's arthritis begins with early diagnosis. The sooner you recognize the subtle symptoms in your dog and have them evaluated by a veterinarian, the sooner treatment can begin. If your dog is diagnosed with arthritis, your veterinarian will prescribe drug treatments aimed at relieving the pain.

A healthy diet and exercise will help your dog maintain optimum health and weight. As a pet owner, your biggest role in managing your dog's arthritis pain is in maintaining good communication with your vet and monitoring your dog's daily behavior. Any changes should be reported to your veterinarian. He may need to adjust or change your dog's medication based on your observations. Love, time together, and your commitment to the general health and well-being of your dog will assure safe and effective arthritis pain treatment and management.

CHAPTER 20: THE RIGHT EXERCISES FOR YOUR DOG'S MIND AND BODY

Keeping an older dog healthy in both mind and body starts with feeding your older dog higher quality food. Good nutritional dog food will keep your dog healthy longer and cut down on your doctor bills. Grocery stores usually sell lower cost dog foods that are lower in quality and are hard for older dogs to digest. Consistency of ingredients and quality can change from one bag to another in grocery store brands.

As your dog gets on in years, he will need quality foods that are high in protein. Higher quality dog foods will usually contain extra vitamins and supplements that will benefit your dog's mental and physical health.

Dogs that are eating poor quality food can often develop diarrhea, vomiting, skin allergies, and experience a loss of energy. The quality of his or her coat will diminish and the shine will disappear. Most bargain brand dog foods are no bargain at all if you have to take your dog to the vet more often. Good quality of life for your dog is worth the extra that you will pay for quality dog food.

Dogs that have reached their senior years may want to sleep the day away and only get moving when they have to go outside or get up for a meal. Older dogs cannot handle the playful activities that they once enjoyed, but they should still be taken out for regular walks. Appropriate exercise benefits dogs by keeping muscles toned and their minds active.

Hearing loss is very common in older dogs and owners should make sure they keep their dogs on a leash when out and about. Old dogs can become confused very quickly with a loss of sight or hearing and may wander off without realizing where they are going. Dog parks are great for dogs to run around and play, but if the park is full of younger dogs, your older dog may not have the energy or interest in the rough play in the park.

Many owners of older dogs find that a training session with their dogs is good for overall fitness. Older dogs can still learn new tricks and commands, and it is a great way to keep the relationship between owner and pet alive. The bonding experience can be fun, but it will depend on your dog's temperament and physical and mental abilities. Finding what motivates your dog to get up and moving is a big plus.

Chapter 21: Why a Massage is Important

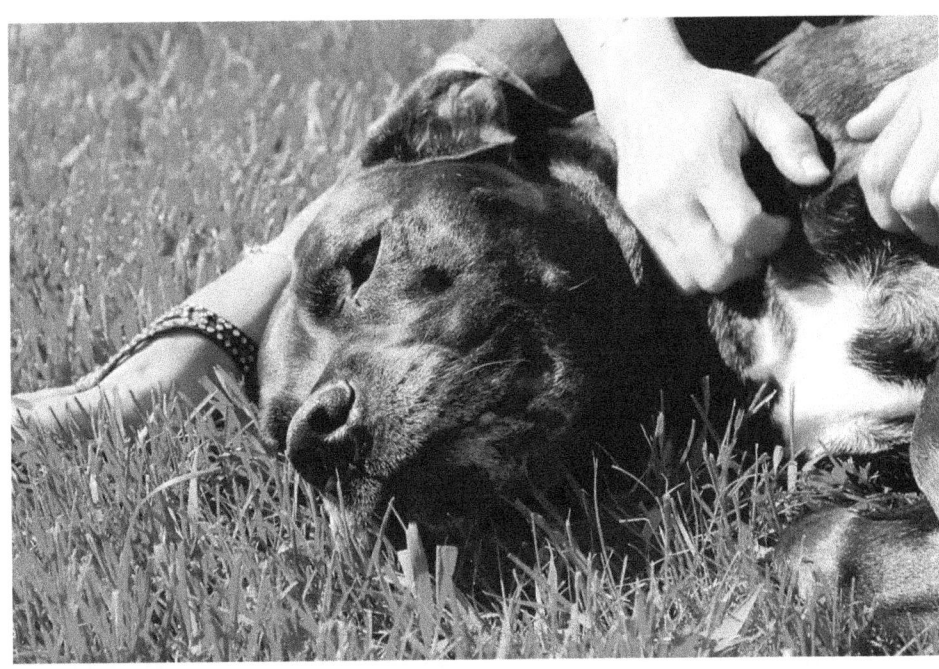

As a valued member of the family, your dog needs your loving care when he or she gets old. Arthritis and other health problems can cause aches and pains, and you can help relieve them with regular massage.

It's Easy to Do

Here are some of the benefits:

- Relieves stiffness and discomfort
- Helps heals soft tissue damage
- Relieves arthritis
- Improves healing
- Helps circulation
- Improved coat

The process is easy. Just follow these simple directions to help your family dog get the relief he or she needs. Begin first by making sure that your dog is comfortable enough to allow you to begin the massage:

- Place a mat on the floor or use your dog's favorite bed.
- Offer some treats for your dog to focus on while you massage.
- Begin by rubbing your thumbs behind the ears of the dog.
- Double-check that your dog is comfortable as you proceed.
- Work down, using your hands, to massage along the sides of the neck.

If the session has gone well, then you can give a deeper massage next time. One excellent massage is the tummy massage. The tummy massage is wonderful for any dog with abdominal distress. It can also help a dog that has difficulty moving his or her bowels. Place towels under your dog before you begin.

- Once the dog is comfortable, with this roll the dog over for a tummy massage.
- Take your hands and move them in a circular motion along the stomach towards the base of the tummy.
- Try not to push too hard as you bring the circular motion back up to the top of the stomach and then down.
- Repeat as needed.

A neck and back massage can help improve the overall health of your dog. Many find it to be an easy because most dogs love to be petted anyway. Make certain that you never straddle the dog. Instead, stand above or to the side and proceed with the massage.

- Take both hands, use the thumbs, and move in a circular motion down the side of the back.
- Continue this back down each time. Try to not work backwards.
- Allow your dog to enjoy this process. Stop if there is any sign of discomfort.
- Work your way through the lower back and smooth out the soft tissue.
- It is best not to add any heat advised by your vet.

Sometimes, as you begin to massage your dog, you will discover injuries that you were unaware of before. Look for cringes of pain as you work your way down the back. This can be a sign of nerve damage or other injuries. It is best to consult your vet before continuing a massage if you notice any signs of pain.

The legs can be massaged in the same way. It's easy, and it allows an older dog a chance to regain needed circulation. Once you find a point of arthritis, then you can help it feel better with regular massage.

- Begin with holding the leg of your dog and stretching it out.
- Bring it back in and repeat this with each leg.

- Take each leg and begin massaging in a circular motion from the base of the hip all the way down to the end of the paw.
- Repeat this with each leg.
- Pay special attention to the tendons and work out any stiffness that you encounter.
- Stop if your dog becomes uncomfortable.

Understand the contact and touch limits of your dog. Some dogs can handle more contact than others. Some might become uncomfortable and require time to get used to the activity.

Massage your dog as often as he or she needs it. Most dogs do not have any problem with massage and come to enjoy it. Your dog's health will benefit from it, too.

CHAPTER 22: GROOMING YOUR OLDER DOG

Elderly dogs that need grooming often suffer from arthritis. A dog's aching bones will be aggravated if it is kept on a grooming table for long periods. Grooming stylists often have older dogs lie or sit down, and ease the pain correlated with a long grooming process.

Several veterinarians and groomers have utilized sling systems marketed towards owners of older dogs, and use these systems to support the dog's hips during grooming. Some physicians recommend putting a sore dog upon its side to trim nails and paw pads, and ease sore joints by reducing overall stress upon the legs. Pulling limbs back can cause great joint strains, and create pain in tendons and muscles. Dogs with hip dysplasia are often treated on their sides to reduce further aches.

Dogs often develop vision disorders as they age, such as cataracts, which may cause formerly calm dogs to become nervous. Dogs with vision impediments may accidentally walk off the grooming table and injure themselves from the fall. Groomers should be careful to maintain constant contact with older dogs in order to assure the animal of its own location. Dogs with cataracts are often more prone to biting out of fear, or moving abruptly during a trim. Dog owners who are aware of these possibilities can prevent injury by utilizing slow, gentle movements. Methodical motions are recommended for any dog. Older dogs can sometimes have impaired hearing so owners should use a gentle approach and show a dog what to expect rather than use verbal commands.

Groomers often find that a pet's skin becomes fragile with age. An elder dog appreciates a light brush, and will find soft movements most comfortable. Owners should use mild shampoos, and use soothing conditioners for their dog's wash, unless otherwise directed by a vet. Some dogs suffer from skin problems, such as thinner skin, and veterinarians may recommend specific treatments in these cases.

Old dogs may sometimes have difficulty tolerating a clipping procedure. The process involves the dog stand upon three legs, and the removal of a dog's support system may cause the dog to fall. For these situations, owners may give their dog a Terrier-style trim, which is both creative and practical for aging dogs.

Professional groomers must communicate a pet's evolving needs to owners. A soft blanket or towel will provide maximum comfort, and ensure a dog remains warm and happy. Some owners might supply a crate for a dog to rest in, and place it within a quieter portion of the shop or grooming area. Dogs must be allowed to take breaks from grooming, and take routine potty breaks outside. Owners should be mindful of outdoor temperatures, and be wary of extreme weather that might upset an older dog.

Owners should utilize delicate and effective drying methods. Owners should also keep cool water within the vicinity, and make sure senior dogs have full access. Senior pets can get cranky and sore, and should be treated quickly. Dogs should be groomed early in the day, and groomers should be finished by mid-afternoon to reduce time away from home or the dog's comfort zone.

Caring for a senior pet is important, and good care is needed for their longevity and happiness. While many senior dogs suffer from poor vision and arthritis, they remain happy in the presence of their owners. Older dogs require love and attention, and above all, should be both clean and presentable, for their happiness and that of their owners.

Meet the Author

Amy and Bruno

Amy Morford has over twenty years of dog training experience with companion dogs, sport dogs and working breeds. Amy's motivation to write about dogs stems from her love for them, and their unbiased loyalty and devotion. Amy's goal is to provide helpful, accurate information to assist dog lovers with raising and training a well-mannered, good-tempered, happy, healthy, well-adjusted companion, friend, partner and/or family pet.

More Books by Amy Morford

Dog Eldercare: Caring For Your Middle-Aged to Older Dog (Dog Care for the Older Canine)

Dog Quotes: Proverbs, Quotes & Quips

How to Speak Dog: Dog Training Simplified For Dog Owners

Pet Names and Numerology: Choose the Right Name For Your Pet

Puppy Training: From Day 1 to Adulthood (How to Make Your Puppy Loving and Obedient)

Scared Dog Audio

The German Shepherd Big Book: All About the German Shepherd Breed

www.ingramcontent.com/pod-product-compliance
Ingram Content Group UK Ltd.
Pitfield, Milton Keynes, MK11 3LW, UK
UKHW050414240426
12048UKWH00020B/1512